我喜欢吃水果和蔬菜

I LOVE TO EAT FRUITS AND VEGETABLES

作者：谢莉·阿德蒙特

插图：索娜·戈亚尔和苏米特·萨库加

www.sachildrensbooks.com
Copyright©2013 by Inna Nusinsky Shmuilov
版权©2013 Inna Nusinsky Shmuilov
innans@gmail.com

All rights reserved. No part of this book may be reproduced in any form or by any electronic or mechanical means, including information storage and retrieval systems, without written permission from the publisher or author, except in the case of a reviewer, who may quote brief passages embodied in critical articles or in a review.

版权所有。
本书的任何一部分都禁止在获取作者许可之前被复制，存储在可检索的系统或者以任何形式，任何工具传递，除非摘录简短的部分用于重要的文章或者报告中。

Translated from English by Jin Ao
翻译：金傲
First edition, 2016

I Love to Eat Fruits and Vegetables (Chinese Englsih Bilingual Edition)/ Shelley Admont
ISBN: 978-1-77268-263-2 paperback
ISBN: 978-1-77268-613-5 hardcover
ISBN: 978-1-77268-262-5 eBook

Please note that the Chinese and English versions of the story have been written to be as close as possible. However, in some cases they differ in order to accommodate nuances and fluidity of each language.

Although the author and the publisher have made every effort to ensure the accuracy and completeness of information contained in this book, we assume no responsibility for errors , inaccuracies, omission or any inconsistency herein.

献给那些我最爱的人

for those I love the most

离午餐还有一个小时。小兔子吉米正在和他的两个哥哥玩耍。
It was an hour before lunch. Jimmy, a little bunny, was playing with his two older brothers.

"我好想吃点甜的东西。"吉米突然说。"或许妈妈那儿有个棒棒糖或 巧克力。"
"I really feel like eating something sweet," said Jimmy suddenly. "Maybe Mom has a lollipop or a piece of chocolate for us."

"午餐前我们不能吃糖果。"大哥说道。"你知道妈妈是不会允许的，吉米。"
"We can't eat candy before lunch," said the oldest brother. "You know we're not allowed, Jimmy."

"我喜欢苹果和葡萄。"二哥说。
"它们又甜又好吃。"
"I like apples and grapes," said the middle brother. "They're sweet and tasty."

吉米撅着嘴。"哼,我不爱吃水果。"
Jimmy curled his lip. "Yuck, I don't like eating fruits."

接着他轻声说道:"你们猜怎么着?我昨天看见妈妈买了些新的糖果。我要去拿一点。谁要和我一起去?"
Then he whispered, "Guess what? I saw that Mom bought some new candy yesterday. I'm going to take some. Who's joining me?"

"我不去。"大哥说完走回去玩他的玩具了。
"Not me," said his oldest brother and went back to his toys.

"我也不去。"二哥回答。
"I'm not coming either," replied his middle brother.

吉米挥了挥手离开了房间。他慢慢地走向厨房，四处打量看有没有被人看见。
Jimmy waved his hand and left the room. Slowly, he made his way to the kitchen, looking around to check that nobody was watching.

餐桌上的午餐都已经准备好了。
The table was already prepared for lunch.

每只兔子都有自己的盘子。大哥的是蓝盘子，二哥的是绿盘子。橘色的盘子是给吉米的。
Each bunny had his own plate. The oldest brother had the blue plate, and the middle brother had the green one. The orange plate was for Jimmy.

桌子中央有一个大碗，碗里都是新鲜的蔬菜。有黄瓜、胡萝卜、番茄、红椒、黄椒还有一些卷心菜。
In the center of the table was a big bowl filled with fresh vegetables. There were cucumbers, carrots, tomatoes, red and yellow peppers, and some cabbage.

吉米皱了皱鼻子。他心想：呕！我才不吃那种东西呢！
Jimmy scrunched his nose. *Ugh! I'm not going to eat THAT,* he thought.

他走向碗柜，发现了装糖果的袋子。但是碗柜太高了，吉米够不着。
He went over to the cupboard and spotted the bag of candy. But the cupboard was so high that Jimmy was unable to reach it.

他搬来一张椅子，拉到碗柜边上。他爬上椅子，但还是够不着架子！
He took one of the chairs and moved it nearer to the cupboard. He climbed up onto it, but he still wasn't able to reach the shelf!

吉米下来，又开始四处看。这回，他拿了一个又大又空的炖锅，把它翻过来。他把锅子放在椅子上然后爬了上去。
Jimmy got back down and looked around again. This time, he took a large empty pot and turned it upside down. He put the pot on the chair and then climbed up.

这次，他能看到最高的架子了。在架子最边上的角落里，有一大袋的糖果！但是……他还是没办法碰到它。他需要再高一点点。
Now, he was able to see the highest shelf. In the far corner of the shelf, there it was a huge bag full of candy! But... he still wasn't able to touch it. He needed to be a tiny bit higher.

我还能用什么呢？吉米一边想一边下来。突然，他看到了妈妈厚厚的烹饪书。
What else can I use? thought Jimmy while getting down. Suddenly, he saw his mom's huge cookbook.

"不就是这个嘛！"他高兴地喊道，抓起书。
"That's exactly what I need!" he said happily as he grabbed the book.

他把烹饪书放在翻过来的炖锅上，慢慢地往上爬。这回他可以碰到架子了。
He put the cookbook on the upside-down pot and slowly climbed up. Now he was able to touch the shelf.

但当吉米去抓糖袋子的时候，椅子开始晃动。吉米失去平衡，摔在地上。
But as Jimmy reached for the bag of candy, the chair began to rock.

吉米失去平衡，摔在地上。
Jimmy quickly lost his balance and fell flat on the ground.

炖锅也掉在他旁边，发出了巨大的响声。接着烹饪书也掉了下来，正好砸在了可怜的吉米的头上。
The pot fell next to him with a loud bang. The cookbook came next, and it landed right on poor Jimmy's head.

"啊呀，好疼！"吉米大叫。他开始觉得有点头晕。
"Ouch, that hurt!" shouted Jimmy. He started feeling a little dizzy.

吉米抬头看碗柜，发现它好像越来越高了。当他试着要站起来的时候，他觉得更晕，只能又坐了回去。
Jimmy looked up at the cupboard and it seemed as if it was getting higher and higher. When he tried to stand up on his feet, he felt dizzier and had to sit back down.

就在这时,他的两个哥哥来到了厨房。"刚刚那是什么声音啊?"大哥问道。"还有吉米呢?"

At that moment, his two older brothers came into the kitchen. "What was that noise," they asked, "and where's Jimmy?"

吉米挥了挥手。"我在这儿！"
Jimmy waved his hand. "I'm here!"

"吉米，你看着……有点不一样。"大哥说。
"你怎么变得这么小了？"二哥问道。
"Jimmy, you look...different," said the oldest brother.
"How did you get so tiny?" asked his middle brother.

这时吉米才意识到为什么别的一切都看起来这么大了。他已经变得和一只老鼠一样小了！
Only then did Jimmy realize why everything looked so big. He had become as small as a mouse!

"我只是爬上去拿点糖果。"他哭着说，"然后我就摔下来了。"
"I just climbed up to get some candy," he cried, "and then I fell down."

"可能就是这样才害你变这么小的！"二哥说道。
"Maybe that's what caused you to become so little!" exclaimed the middle brother.

"哦，不！我会一直这么小吗？"吉米开始哭了。
"Oh, no! Will I stay this small forever?" Jimmy began crying.

"别哭了。"大哥说。"我们会想出办法的。我们先在妈妈进来前打扫干净吧。"
"Don't cry," said the oldest brother. "We will figure something out. Let's just clean up before Mom comes in."

当他们刚把所有东西都归位时，他们的妈妈走进了厨房。
Just as they finished putting everything back in its place, their mother walked into the kitchen.

"我们马上要准备吃午餐了。吉米去哪儿了？"吉米躲在哥哥们的后面。
"We're going to eat lunch soon. Where's Jimmy?" Jimmy hid behind his older brothers.

"呃、呃……"二哥吞吞吐吐,不知道该怎么说。
"Uh, uh..." stuttered his middle brother while thinking of something to say.

但是大哥很聪明。
But the older brother was very smart.

"妈妈,如果有人想快快长大,变得又高又壮,他该怎么做呢?"他问道。

"Mom, if someone wants to grow quickly and be tall and strong, what would he need to do?" he asked.

"他需要吃水果和蔬菜。"妈妈回答道。"水果和蔬菜含有丰富的维他命和矿物质,帮助身体更快地成长。"
"He needs to eat his fruits and vegetables," she answered. "They contain lots of vitamins and minerals that help the body grow faster."

"现在,你们可以在座位上坐好,我去叫爸爸和吉米。"妈妈说完走出了厨房。
"Now, you can sit down at the table and I will call Dad and Jimmy," their mother said and walked out of the kitchen.

大哥转向吉米。"快点!你得吃水果和蔬菜。"
The oldest brother turned around to Jimmy. "Quick! You have to eat your fruits and vegetables."

"没门!"吉米尖叫。"我不喜欢水果和蔬菜!"
"No way!" screamed Jimmy, "I don't even like fruits or vegetables!"

"你想一辈子都这个样子吗？"他的二哥问道。
"Do you want to stay this way forever then?" his middle brother asked.

"当然不想！"吉米说。
"Of course not!" replied Jimmy.

"所以吃点蔬菜。"大哥说。"说不能你会喜欢呢。"
"So eat some vegetables," said the oldest brother. "Maybe you'll even like them."

他从桌上的碗里拿了一根胡萝卜，塞进吉米的嘴里。
He took a carrot from the bowl on the table and slipped it in Jimmy's mouth.

"唔……它甜甜的，很好吃。"吉米一边说，一边用自己坚固的、洁白的牙齿咀嚼胡萝卜。
"Ummm...this is sweet and tasty," Jimmy said as he chewed his carrot with his strong, white teeth.

就在这时，他觉得一股奇怪的刺痛感传遍全身——就像魔术一样。他的腿变得更强壮，他甚至变高了一点。
All of the sudden, he felt a strange tingly feeling spreading all over his body—it was just like magic. His legs got stronger, and he even became a little taller.

"吉米，看！你已经长大一点了！"大哥大叫道。
"Jimmy, look! You've grown a bit!" shouted the oldest brother.

二哥从碗里给吉米拿了一根多汁的黄瓜。"给，吃点别的。"他说。
The middle brother gave Jimmy a juicy cucumber from the bowl. "Here, eat something else," he said.

每吃一口，吉米感觉身体越来越强壮，他在长个儿！
With every bite, he felt his body getting stronger and stronger. He was growing!

"你终于变回你自己了。"大哥叫着,跑向吉米,拥抱他。
"You're finally yourself again," the oldest brother shouted and ran over to hug Jimmy.

他的二哥也拥抱他。"你现在觉得怎么样?"他问道。
His middle brother hugged him, too. "How are you feeling now?" he asked.

"我觉得好极了,浑身充满了能量。"吉米回答说。"你猜怎么着?这些水果和蔬菜真的太好吃了。我以前就该早点尝尝看的!"
"I feel great and full of energy," Jimmy answered. "And you know what? These fruits and vegetables are really tasty. I should have tried them before!"

三兄弟开始放声大笑,跳来跳去。
All three brothers began to laugh loudly and jump around.

几分钟后，吉米的父母走进了厨房。
A few minutes later, Jimmy's parents entered the kitchen.

"太好了，你在这儿。"爸爸说。
"Great, everyone's here," said Dad.

"看到每个人心情都这么好，我真是太开心了。"妈妈说。"就这么愉快地开始吃午餐吧！别忘了先洗手哦！"
"I'm happy that everyone's in such a good mood," said Mom. "What a great way for us to start lunch! Don't forget to wash your hands!"

这个快乐的家庭围坐在大桌边，开始品尝美食。连吉米也吃得一干二净。
The happy family sat around the large table and began eating all the tasty things there. Even Jimmy finished his whole plateful.

从那天起,吉米喜欢上了吃所有的水果和蔬菜。有时候,他还是吃糖果,但是只吃一点点,还是在吃完饭之后才吃。

From that day on, Jimmy liked eating all his fruits and vegetables. Sometimes, he still ate candy but only a little and only after his meals.

CPSIA information can be obtained
at www.ICGtesting.com
Printed in the USA
LVHW072154130421
684402LV00008B/308